THE BRETHREN Spirit

ROBERT C SMITH

BALBOA
PRESS
A DIVISION OF HAY HOUSE

Copyright © 2015, 2016 ROBERT C SMITH.

All rights reserved. No part of this book may be used or reproduced by any means, graphic, electronic, or mechanical, including photocopying, recording, taping or by any information storage retrieval system without the written permission of the author except in the case of brief quotations embodied in critical articles and reviews.

Balboa Press books may be ordered through booksellers or by contacting:

Balboa Press
A Division of Hay House
1663 Liberty Drive
Bloomington, IN 47403
www.balboapress.com
1 (877) 407-4847

Because of the dynamic nature of the Internet, any web addresses or links contained in this book may have changed since publication and may no longer be valid. The views expressed in this work are solely those of the author and do not necessarily reflect the views of the publisher, and the publisher hereby disclaims any responsibility for them.

The author of this book does not dispense medical advice or prescribe the use of any technique as a form of treatment for physical, emotional, or medical problems without the advice of a physician, either directly or indirectly. The intent of the author is only to offer information of a general nature to help you in your quest for emotional and spiritual well-being. In the event you use any of the information in this book for yourself, which is your constitutional right, the author and the publisher assume no responsibility for your actions.

Any people depicted in stock imagery provided by Thinkstock are models, and such images are being used for illustrative purposes only.
Certain stock imagery © Thinkstock.

Print information available on the last page.

ISBN: 978-1-5043-4745-7 (sc)
ISBN: 978-1-5043-4747-1 (hc)
ISBN: 978-1-5043-4746-4 (e)

Library of Congress Control Number: 2015921288

Balboa Press rev. date: 1/13/2016

Contents

Acknowledgements ix
The Circle of Light Spiritualist Church xi
Foreword xiii

Part 1: My Formative Years in
Religion and Spiritual Awareness 1

    My Spiritual Awakening 5
    Tony Blackmore Trance Mediumship 7
    Sue Rose, Medium 8
    The Soul of a Pyramid 10
    Reading Our Souls 10
    A Mediums' Work 11
    Birth Chart Interpretation by Sue White 12

Part 2: My Spiritual Philosophy 16

    My Children 17
    The Font of All Knowledge 18
    Soul Searching 19
    Personal Development 20
    Everyday Life 21
    Seeds of Time 22
    New Beginnings 23
    Light Workers 24
    Messages from the Heart 25
    The Beauty of the Mind 26

Drinking from the Well	27
The Brotherhood of Man	28
The Twelve Chakras	29
The Communicator	30
Guardian Angel	31
Crystals	32
Upliftment	34
Progress of a Medium	35
Love Divine	36
Reincarnation of the Spirit	37
Our Friends	38
The Colour Yellow	40
A Pink Bubble	40
Autumn Leaves	41
Grandparents	42
A New-born Baby	44
My Archangel	45
Dreams	46
One Small Step	47
Christmas	48
A Child Is Born	49
Our Faith	50
A Place for Us	51
The Spiritual Connection	52
The Colour Green	53
The Colour Purple	54
Memories	56
Inspiration	57
Springtime	58
Love	59

Planet Earth 61
Your Grandmother 62
The Light 63
The Soul 64
Dream Travel 65
The Elements 66
Beings of Light 68
The Flowers 69
Life Eternal 70
Archangel Michael 71
Free Will 73
The Light Shines within Us 74
Understanding 75
Spirituality 76
Spiritual Direction and Meaning 77
Healing 78

Part 3: Guides, Past Life Regression, Trance Mediumship. 81

My Guide Karis 81
Illumination of Ray 14 81
Past Life Regression by Delyse Bastista-Pedro 82
Past Life Regression by Jeff Powell
(First Regression) 83
Past Life Regression by Jeff Powell
(Second Regression) 84
Dream Experiences and Outcomes 84
Trance Mediumship with Tony Blackmore 1 86
Trance Mediumship with Tony Blackmore 2 88

Part 4: Poems and Meditations 90

- Meditation: Atlantis 90
- Poem of Love 92
- Meditation with the White Brethren 92
- Meditation for Forgiveness 94
- Meditation Following a House Clearance 95
- A Prayer for Love 96
- Spring Has Sprung 97
- The Daffodil 98
- Divine Timing by Sue for Robert 98
- The Unicorn by Joseph Panek 99

Appendix 101
Resources 103

Acknowledgements

"I extend my heartfelt gratitude to the following people for the support and encouragement given to me during my Spiritual path and lifetime achievements".

Maxine Mustoe Is a Spiritual medium who works with nature and the angels, for writing an inspiring foreword to this book.

Rev Phil Phillips, medium, for his inspiration, for training me to become a healer, and for leading me onto the spiritual path.

Rev Anthony Blackmore, trance medium, for his dedication to Spirit, for the experience of a lifetime, and for his encouragement for me to write this book.

Sue Rose, medium, for taking me on after Tony passed over to Spirit and for her professional guidance, love, and support in pushing my writing career forward.

The Circle of Light Spiritualist Church – my thanks to all the mediums who have worked with Spirit over the years and all the people that I have been associated with, and to all our members who have supported me and our Church.

Christopher Hunter Worrall Medium for supporting me in my writing and for being a source of inspiration.

The Corinthian Church and Healing Association for showing me the spiritual path and for supporting me on my healing career.

Jeff Powell's Past Life Regression Workshop for bringing my past life experiences forward in 2010.

Delyse Bastista-Pedro for the past life regression as a Roman centurion after our healing sessions.

Sue White for producing my birth chart, which pinpoints my psychic and intuitive skills.

Marcus Burnett, spiritual medium and psychic artist, who created the mural.

My parents, Charlie and Dorothy; my grandparents, Henry and Violetta, Rees and Celia Ann; together with all my other relatives in Spirit for their endless messages of love and support on the other side of the veil.

For my two sons and their families: Oliver and Melissa, along with Araminta, my first granddaughter; Toby and Henrietta, along with Phoebe, my second granddaughter – my thanks for being there for me, with all the *love* from a proud father and grandfather.

The Circle of Light Spiritualist Church

The membership of our church has built up over the years, and today it has a good following. Even though the premises have changed owners several times, the support is there for everyone to see. Most people who come to services are looking for answers just as I did back in the nineties.

The loss of a loved one through old age, a sudden accident, or an ongoing illness is always hard to bear. There are many types of cancer, a stroke, a heart attack, motor-neuron disease, Alzheimer's, or an aneurism are all things that sometimes shorten people's lives or take them when we least expect them to pass over.

These people are going through a period of grief, wanting to know whether their nearest and dearest are with their loved ones in the spirit world. A message from a loved one in spirit can do wonders for one's own self-esteem and eliminate worry from one's mind, when he or she is looking for proof, answers, and reassurance that the loved ones are still around.

For example, Marj came to our church several years ago. She had a son called Martin, aged 16, a likeable lad who underneath was sensitive but was always smiling. Unfortunately he was bullied at school for twelve years. Even though other parents and school teachers did what they could, the problem would not go away. The policies available at that time did not give the teachers adequate instruction in how to deal with bullying. Martin never talked in detail or in depth about the bullying, and he feared retaliation from those who were bullying him, so the magnitude did not become apparent until after he took his own life.

Since then Marj and her family have looked for ways to overcome their grief. They have found that counselling and regular attendance at our church have brought them healing emotionally, mentally, and spiritually. In the friendly, family atmosphere with like-minded people who attend our church, they are all finding peace of mind and acceptance of loved ones in Spirit.

Marj and her supporters now raise money for Papyrus, a national charity dedicated to the prevention of young suicide, founded in 1997 by a group of parents who had lost a child. Their helpline is a unique service that can be called in the UK at 0800 065 4141; text messages can be sent to 0778 620 9697, and emails to pat@papyrus-uk.org.

Foreword

By Maxine Mustoe

Since the age of 6, I have learnt and borne witness as a spiritual medium that there are a host of benevolent beings from other-worldly dimensions. As we travel through the earthly years of our lives, these light beings are more than willing to guide and support us.

Ultimately, we shall make our own choices, be they right or wrong, but always those loving and often invisible hands will hold us close. I have been assured by my own spirit guide that we will never be judged either way for what we decide.

Like me, you are on a quest to find knowledge you can trust that is woven in truth and fused with the purest of love. I found a precious gift of hope, brought into being by my dear friend and colleague Robert Smith. He channelled the wonderful philosophy within the pages of this book. The guidance transcends time and relativity, taking us back into the arms of innocence and to the inner child within us all. It is from this perspective that we can reconfigure our sometimes fraught pathways and align back with the Divine.

Robert's soul searching came after the death of his beloved parents in the late 1980s. Throwing his thoughts out into the universe, he asked, "Where have they gone?" His journey took him to an adorable little church, tucked into a quaint countryside lane. It was here he met his friend, mentor, and teacher, Tony Blackmore.

Robert went from the congregation to become a healer, graduating from the Corinthian Church and Healing Association. But it soon became clear to Tony through his own guides that Robert had another mission ahead of him in terms of fulfilling his passion as a healer. Invited by his teacher to attend a spiritual development circle, Robert felt inspired to bring a pen and paper to the sessions. It did not take long for the pages to become filled with the most beautiful words, embellished with a healing vibration.

I have been privileged over the years, whilst serving that church and the one that Robert now runs, to follow and witness the unfolding of wisdom and love this work has achieved.

Karis, one of Robert's spirit guides, who helped in the making of this book, reminds us all of our self-worth and encourages us to find our unique gifts. He says, "Every child that comes to our earth plains is a gift from the spiritual world, to grow, learn, follow the paths of righteousness, and achieve his or her aims and obligations in life."

Part 1

My Formative Years in Religion and Spiritual Awareness

My first impressions of religion were formed in my early years, starting at the age of 5, in the Anglican Church. I attended my family's first church in Chittoe, Wiltshire, when I was about 10 years old. My mother was a very keen churchgoer, and the four of us regularly attended church three times on a Sunday – Morning Prayer, Sunday school in the afternoon, and Evensong at six o'clock. It did not matter to me, because I always felt good every time I went to church. I was part of the choir, along with my sister, and we both sang well. There was something special about going to this church. There was a feeling of spiritual awareness that was special whenever we attended services.

Like many people, music was inspirational to me, especially classical music like Tchaikovsky and Rimsky-Korsakov. I was interested in violin music and was learning to play during my teenage years at a music school in Calne, Wiltshire. Unfortunately, when I was 14 years of age, my father took a job in Gloucestershire, which meant that we all moved with him, and it was difficult to find a music tutor in the new area. But my interest in music has not dwindled.

I still enjoy concerts, and symphony orchestral music can be so very uplifting and rewarding.

During this time, having changed to a new school and another form of teaching in Bourton-on-the-Water, my sister and I needed some adjustment. We were at that time attending a new church in Little Rissington, where we lived. It was called St Peter's. It was not long before we were both confirmed in this church, along with others in the village, by the bishop of Gloucester, David Asquith. This meant we could now attend communion services and receive communion.

Having had a good upbringing from my parents, my path was laid out for me – a moral and religious life that included getting a vocation in electrical engineering and attending college one day a week as part of my apprenticeship. I also had sporting activities like football, cricket, and athletics. I was quite fanatical about taking part and being a member of a team. I always felt the right combination and the camaraderie was the right ingredient.

Up to the age of twenty-seven, I made great progress in the electrical field in the United Kingdom, so I had had an attractive résumé. To further my career, I decided to go to Australia, because I was interested in travel and in learning how people lived in such a vast country. Within a year, my qualifications allowed me to secure a job in northwest Australia as a supervisor on the construction of an iron-ore project. I was a member of the electrical engineering construction team, working for a major international company called Bechtel Pacific Corporation. The workforce consisted of five hundred men of all nationalities, who lived in air-conditioned accommodations at the port site. There was not much to do in our spare time, so I became the cinema operator and showed films flown up from Perth during the week. Every eight weeks, we were allowed a long weekend in Perth to recharge our batteries and stay with our friends.

After three years, the project was coming to an end, and the feeling of being away from England was drawing me back. My father was not in good health, and the need to return was strong. When I did arrive back home, my father was admitted to hospital for an operation that had a recovery time of nine months. During his absence, I was able to carry out his work until he was fit enough to return to work.

At this time, I was a self-employed electrician, and my workload was increasing, so I set up my own electrical-contracting business. I employed a man to assist me in our workload, but after a few years, he decided to return to Ireland for family reasons.

The business took a different direction when I became involved in the installation work for automated feeding systems for dairy cows throughout the country. As this was a new electronic system, there were a few teething problems to be sorted along the way. Altogether, it turned out a success.

It was not long before an international company sought my services to cover automated feeding systems for chickens, ducks, geese, cattle, calves, pigs, and battery hens. This was a European venture by an American company named Chore Time, which was based in Belgium. My job was to service the United Kingdom, Ireland, Denmark, Sweden, Yugoslavia, and Greece, so I had lots of traveling to do and was away from home most weeks.

At this particular time, I was married to Jane and we were expecting our first child. It just so happened that I was in Denmark when I got the call that Jane was in Bristol's Southmead Hospital and I needed to get there as fast as possible. I immediately took a flight to Newcastle then another to Birmingham and finally a car to Bristol. The birth of Oliver happened on February 2, 1982, and he was put into an incubator because he had developed jaundice. All went well, and after a few days, both mother and child were allowed home. Eighteen months later, our second son, Toby, was born on August 17, 1983 in Southmead Hospital. He had the same condition, but after the same treatment, he was allowed home a few days later.

The strain of traveling with my work and being away from home was not good for my family life, so a change in my occupation was necessary. I secured a job with Babcock Electrical Projects in Gloucester. This meant having my family life back together, and over the next few years we enjoyed holiday's abroad and visited places in Cornwall, Devon, Yorkshire, Scotland,

and Dorset. Life was very enjoyable, and the boys were growing in stature.

Our first home in this area was built by a local builder in natural Cotswold stone. I completed the interior with the help of other subcontractors over a period of two years; because I was so busy traveling and working abroad. The second home was also new and was built in reconstituted stone in Bourton-on-the-Water, an idyllic place and a busy tourist village in the Cotswolds. But we did not get to live in this house, because an old property became available in the village, and my wife wanted us to move into it. That place had a lot of character, including a barn and stables with a good-sized garden for the boys to play in. It was here they learned to ride their bikes. After a couple of years this was all about to change. In 1987 my father passed away suddenly from an aneurism close to his heart.

My Spiritual Awakening

Following the passing of my parents – my father in 1987 and my mother in 1992 – my thoughts led me to seek answers to questions like this: "Where have they gone after passing to the other side of life?"

My first step was to seek a medium called Reverend Phil Phillips at the Corinthian Spiritualist Church and Healing Association at Uckington, Cheltenham. Phil gave me a reading and brought through both of my parents, who assured me they were all right, that they loved me, and that they would be around me whenever I needed them. Phil also gave me validation from my parents, who told me things that only I knew. It was a very emotional reading, and the tears flowed with love and joy in knowing that they were together and that life continues in the spirit world.

My interest in the Spiritualist Church widened, and soon I was attending weekly services at the Evergreen as it was called in those early days and is now known as The Circle of Light. After a while, Phil started up a training course in healing for six people through the Corinthian Church. We each were given a training manual consisting of the following:

- an introduction to healing
- the human aura and chakra system
- distant or absent healing
- attunement
- a typical healing session
- confidentiality and keeping records
- an introduction to counselling/listening skills
- a basic introduction to anatomy and physiology
- meditation
- protection
- visualization
- the causes of illness
- final topics (personal hygiene, diagnosis, and running a clinic)

The training course ran for six months and was followed by a further twelve months as a probation healer with acceptance by the Corinthian Church, together with a certificate issued in April 1999. For this, I have to thank Phil and Jenny for their dedication and expertise in teaching us as a group to become proficient healers. An open circle was established within the church on a separate evening when we practised meditation, breathing exercises, opening of chakras, connecting with our guides, and seeing colours, people, places, buildings, and landscapes. Healing continued for members of the church for many years, until Phil decided to move to pastures new.

Tony Blackmore Trance Mediumship

We have sat many times since 2009 in a Tony Blackmore closed circle. Usually there are six of us each week. There has been a lot of love, laughter, and leg-pulling in our spiritual work, especially when Tony goes into a trance. I shall withhold his doorkeeper's name out of respect. We enjoyed him immensely. It was his job to bring forward a communicator who would be suitable for the required level in our spiritual advancement. Sometimes it would be a high-profile figure such as Oscar Wilde or a guide from the higher realms.

In each of our messages, we would be given some information that would enhance our spiritual paths.

These messages raised our vibrations, and over time the information has come to fruition.

They were happy times sitting in Tony's closed circle. He had a marvellous sense of humour. Our own personalities blended with his, and we looked forward to meeting up every week. But Tony was a strong disciplinarian who pulled anyone up if they had stepped out of line, Tony was a good tutor, and he taught us very well. His meditations brought out the best in us, and his regime in conducting spiritual work was dedicated. Some of the meditations are listed in the Table of Contents and appear in this book.

It was a big disappointment to us all when Tony's health deteriorated and he felt he could not carry on with our closed circle. Eventually Tony got his wish and passed over to be with his loved ones in Spirit. We and his friends gave him a good send off.

Sue Rose, Medium

Before he went, Tony did pass me on to another medium called Sue Rose, for which I was most grateful. Sue has a wonderful tenderness when working with Spirit, and she likes to work with about six of us each week in a closed circle. We are set different tasks each week – to write or draw about such things as linking with our guides and archangels, good intentions, meditations, linking with another person in the group, reading auras, tuning into colours, and mind energy. My aura consists of purple and blue. The colour purple is circulating around my head and shoulders. This is very helpful when doing healing and spiritual growth. The colour blue is around the neck area and aids communication on all levels. It is also my favourite colour, which gives me clarity when writing. This is the one area that satisfies me the most, and words come from profound knowledge in several spheres. It is my foremost gift in spiritual work, and it inspires me to write more and also inspires others when giving a reading.

After sitting in circle for some years now, I have come to the conclusion that working with Spirit can be one of the most rewarding things one can do. When one brings forward a message to a loved one on the earth plains, it can be gratefully received with love and admiration. There are several ways a medium can work with Spirit. In my case, writing to channel the information is my chosen path, because I get the most satisfaction from it. The spiritual link between humans and our loved ones in spirit gives us the balance between our material and spiritual lives, and by doing this, we are leading a better life between the two worlds.

The Soul of a Pyramid

Another subject was to draw and write about a pyramid and how we use the light. The pyramid reflects the light like a human being, the inner energy coming from the sun or the moon to give light by and from reflections from the universe and the earth. The colours are varied and are seen in different dimensions, especially in the night-time sky. A pyramid is not just a symbol or a resting place for Pharaohs in Egypt but a beacon that transmits light either to the universe or to another trig point upon the earth. We may not fully understand its purpose, for we should look at it as a soul that lives within and serves a purpose beyond our realm of comprehension. We will never cease to wonder at man's inventions and never doubt the inspiration given to us from a higher level.

Reading Our Souls

The connection of your soul is one of divine and celestial being to the universe. The soul is an everlasting life that lives in eternity throughout many generations.

The true meaning of a soul cannot be measured in the number of lifetimes the soul returns to earth or other planets. The soul returns to earth to accumulate knowledge from past lives and is known as a wise old soul.

The connection builds up a vast amount of knowledge over the soul and excursions to the brain is of the most importance for us to survive. Our human lives are led by what we get from our souls' past experiences. We can learn many things that the soul imparts to our brain, thereby acting as an advisor. Although we have difficulty listening to our soul, we should always remember that our soul is part of us and will always be with us.

A Mediums' Work

A medium's work with Spirit has to be one that you as an individual desire to perform. The connection forms a link between your guide and yourself. The will from you to work as a medium is a commitment with Spirit to bring satisfaction from yourself to the intended receiver. The validation of the person you are linking with requires some evidence that the receiver will recognise a relative or a loved one. In all cases, we are bringing receivers on the earth plains closer to their loved ones in Spirit. Our contact with Spirit can be channelled in several ways, including sensing, feeling, clairaudience, and clairsentience, and to master any of these channels takes time through meditation to connect and channel the intended message from

Spirit. The satisfaction is reflected in the delivery and content by the medium and the receiver of the message. It is only then that a medium will feel satisfaction in carrying out the delivery between the two worlds.

Birth Chart Interpretation by Sue White

Robert is a sun-sign Aquarius, with the moon also in Aquarius. The ascendant is in Scorpio and midheaven in Virgo. This combination is very powerful, giving a personality of considerable force. With the Scorpio ascendant, it is probable that you are an "old soul" with many lifetimes experience on earth and a great deal of spiritual knowledge. Scorpio ascendant is a very intense influence and gives the type of personality that often undergoes sudden changes and devastating events which revolutionizes that life. Such subjects often lose everything or leave everything behind them. Although you might plunge into the depths of despair during such times, you have the ability to jump back and to completely recover very quickly. You have stamina and good regenerative powers.

The Aquarius sun and moon give independence and a love of freedom. It is humanitarian and sociable (in a detached way) and could be quite political. You could be involved in fighting for better conditions for others or representing others in some way. Because you are caring and yet detached, you are good at that sort of thing. However, if you do become personally involved, you can (Scorpio ascendant) become *very* attached and involved. You have the capacity for both responses. You are also likely to be technically minded. The sun is in Fourth House, so home and home affairs are important to you. The sun is conjunct Mercury, which tells me that you are good at communication with others. The moon is carrying many aspects and says that you have a lot of different emotional responses. You are emotionally mature and responsible and are good at actively caring for others. You are a busy person with considerable courage and the ability to act on your own initiative. If necessary, you can express your feelings with considerable force – possibly even physical force. You are probably attracted to strong women. You could be quite highly strung and find it hard to relax. You are more sensitive than people imagine and could be quite touchy.

With the moon square Uranus, you are extremely independent and freedom loving, which could be difficult in relationships. The Venus placing is very good. Workwise you are a wise handler of money and prudent. You are a good team worker and have good relationships with authority figures, although you would stand your ground if something was wrong and needed to be addressed. There could have been a certain lack of self-worth and fear of rejection when you were young. However, with maturity you have gained a responsible position, which has improved your feelings of self-worth. You have a reckless side, although you are usually very sensible. You have some Mars connections, which one might expect to; see in a military person's chart. There is a great driving force which will override others if necessary and the capacity to take charge and to take risks. Mars trine Saturn makes you tough and determined, with great stamina. There is a creative ability and also technical skills, which could make you good at technical drawing or the like. There is also a lot to say: you are psychic and intuitive. (Surprise, Surprise!)

There are a couple of T-square patterns, which give tension and pressure in certain areas. The first one has the moon (emotions) at the crux and produces extreme sensitivity with emotional relationships. Because of this, relationships could be many and short-lived. The lesson here is to be more "laid back" about relationships and to focus your mind on ninth-house activities (in astrological terms) – that is, on higher-mind activities, with your north node in Scorpio in the twelfth house. Spiritual and psychic development is very much your path, and someone who shares this interest would obviously be the best match. Your ideal mate would be a Taurus type, i.e., someone well grounded, practical, and steady, with a caring nature. The other T-square pattern links Mars, Jupiter, and the midheaven. There is extreme force and ambition here, which could overreach one. It is a lesson to curb extreme ambition and to keep moderation in mind.

To balance the tension of these two patterns, there is a lovely grand trine between Venus, Uranus, and the M.C. This is free-flowing, easy energy, which makes it simple for you to cooperate with others and to be carefree and flexible. There are two non-aspected planets: Neptune and Pluto. These are both planets that tell us of your deep-seated, psychological urges. Aspects from other planets give outlets and paths of expression for the very powerful energies that these planets produce. Without aspects, the energies can become clammed up and then explode without warning into sudden outbursts. These placing are very good for psychic work. The work itself can be a channel for release of the pent-up energy, and any type of creative or artistic work will also serve as an outlet, as will robust but creative physical work like gardening. It is important always to have one or more of these outlets, or you could feel tense, aggressive, or depressed.

Part 2

My Spiritual Philosophy

My Children

All of the people on the earth plains are my children. They are part of the creation of mankind, to live and work together for the benefit of the planet across all faiths and religions, to live in peace and harmony.

The purpose of the planet earth was to show a land of peace, goodwill, and abundance for all who subscribed to the cause of living and working together in one aim, but over the years war and tensions between men and countries in search of power and conquest have blighted man's thinking in favour of greed, selfishness, and control over other people.

This has led to much suffering and pain for many people, who cannot see the reason for such actions.

In order to address the situation, mankind has to eliminate power, greed, and selfishness and work together for the common good to restore planet earth to its true potential – that of a land that was meant for people to live and enjoy together in a community spirit, all working for one another.

By working and sharing the fruits and crops to provide for families, by making household items from wood, by creating pottery by hand, by blowing glass to use as drinking vessels, and by women creating clothes from spinning and pattern making, everyone contributes towards providing a service to others in their community and is paid in the barter system of trading.

In this way families will feel more self-sufficient in providing and contributing to their societies and will live a non-materialistic and spiritual life

The Font of All Knowledge

Intentions are what we want to achieve in goodness and light, so that we direct our pathways into satisfaction and progress.

We have an abundance of knowledge at our disposal, and we must tap into this reservoir to enhance our skills in demonstrating our ability to link with Spirit and channel the messages of love and support to those that require uplifting in their hour of sorrow, grief, or depression.

Ours is the need to give sympathy, support, and love so that our friends become stronger and more enlightened in facing their difficulties, however great or small they may be.

Each one of us is a special individual and is not duplicated in any form upon the earth. We are unique as people, because we were each born at a time and place that cannot be replicated by anyone else.

Each of us has different skills, ideas, dreams, and fantasies, that make us a special person, capable of sharing, caring, loving, giving, and bonding to each other so that we may fulfil the potential of our lives.

In the time we have been given to live our life upon the earth plains, we need to achieve several goals that we agreed to before we came here. It is up to each one of us to ensure that we do this before we move onto another life or another planet to fulfil our obligations.

Soul Searching

At some times in our lives we connect with another soul from a previous life who may still work with us in our current life. These are called old souls, and they have been with us over a great many years.

These souls are the ones who have great wisdom and clarity in their messages to remind us of the path that we tread.

We are reminded countless times to connect with our angels, archangels, and guides, who are there for us whenever we need them. Theirs is a devoted love for those who seek them.

Throughout our lives there has always been a time when we have needed them, because we have come to a crossroads or have suffered pain, anguish, and sorrow due to the loss of a loved one who walked on the same path with us and who is forever in our hearts.

At other times we have searched for soul mates on the earth plains, people who have a mutual understanding, affection, love, and companionship that enriches our lives, especially if the bond is made through our family life, our wife or partner, and our children too. It is this desire within each of us to satisfy our soul, knowing that we have served God's purpose for us on earth.

At the conclusion of our life on earth, our soul returns to the spirit world, and all souls are rejoicing in being together again.

Personal Development

Let the light shine forth on the chosen few that they can be fulfilled in carrying out their chosen path in the ways that they feel most comfortable with. After all, we work from the heart with love, compassion, and support for those who seek peace of mind, a connection with the higher life, and gratification of the soul in order to maintain the balance between the physical and spiritual paths that we live.

It is a journey that was predicted at the beginning of our life here on earth, and although we may not realise it for many years, we eventually know what our purpose is and proceed to work with Spirit, angels, archangels, guides, helpers, and family members to bring the connection of the two worlds together.

In order to achieve this potential, we must strive to accomplish the skills, direction, discipline, and the truth in conveying the words of comfort, love, free will, and dedication to bring a joyful reunion between the family, friends, and acquaintances of the loved one.

In doing this we will have achieved our chosen path to carry out the bond with the ones we love.

Everyday Life

We welcome the spiritual light into our minds to enhance our knowledge of learning and to accept the wisdom of our spiritual guides in furthering our path towards the connection of the two worlds.

We have before us obstacles, trials, and tribulations that are meant to test us. Some of them are painful, to the point where a harsh lesson has to be learnt in order to progress.

In the loss of a loved one, we endure sorrow, loneliness, isolation, and fear of being separated, but in time we grow stronger and learn to adapt our way of living with our friends and family.

The path of contentment lies in our belief to overcome adversities, follow our intuition, and believe in ourselves,

Grow stronger and have faith. Support one another, fill your daily lives with like-minded people, take on new challenges, be positive in everything you do, help someone in need, and be kind in thought word and deed.

Make allowances for those less fortunate than yourself. Make amends with those friends you have fallen out with. Make a pact to work together in love, peace, and harmony.

Seeds of Time

The seeds of time were planted many years ago, and they roll on forever. Time is measured in our daily lives in everything we do. It seems to control our lives in determining what time we spend eating, sleeping, working, and playing.

We have the capacity to fill our lives with so many things of a practical or intellectual nature, and yet it can take several years before we acknowledge our spiritual life awareness, which in itself is beyond time when we communicate with our loved ones.

Throughout our time we strive to achieve pinnacles of status, position, and authority as measured by our success. We believe that this is our chosen path when we have achieved our goals, but when we do reach this point, we realise there is something else that we have overlooked. That is our spiritual life, which has so much more meaning, acceptance, quality of life, purpose, and well-being to fulfil our lives.

To live as one with one common denominator, we can enrich our lives with love and compassion towards our fellow man and fellow woman, our family and friends.

Be as one and soak up the sands of time.

New Beginnings

The joys of spring bring forward a freshness that is uplifting when the flowers appear and blossom. The snowdrops, daffodils, lilies of the valley, primroses, and bluebells are bringing life to us all, following the drab winter of frost, snow, wind, and rain.

Now is the time to replenish our souls with vigour and vitality, to welcome the sun on our faces that gives us a glow of satisfaction.

Now is the time for the birds to sing and busy themselves with pairing and nest building to rear their young, feeding and protecting them.

The same applies to the human race. It's all part of evolution – man, woman, and child – to continue life's cycle, to progress, to recreate our lives on this planet, to maintain the ecology of our plant and tree life, and to maintain a consistent growth of beauty and a continuation of all species for our offspring and their families.

We are the caretakers to ensure we have the stability, creativity, longevity, sensibility, and capability to carry out the responsibilities before us.

It is within each and every one of us to make sure that our planet is nourished, replenished, protected, and fortified for all mankind.

Light Workers

Every day we have the opportunity to walk in the light, whether it is for meditation, healing, praying, or mediumship working with angels and archangels.

By some we are looked upon as being light workers who give their time to link with the spiritual world, to enhance and embrace all those that we come into contact with and spread the light and the love.

By giving of ourselves to others, we are fulfilling our obligation to the spirit world and those within it.

We are at our most happiness when we achieve the link, transfer the messages, healing, light, and love to those who need it most.

When we lose a loved one to the spirit world, we feel sorrow and mourn, but when our soul passes to the spirit world, much rejoicing and happiness abounds, because we have returned home.

The passage of time that we spend on the earth plains is for us a time to learn and overcome difficulties however painful they may be.

Our life on earth is what some would call a learning curve with challenges, obstacles, and pitfalls, and it is for each one of us to overcome that which is put before us with discipline, dedication, and determination.

In essence, it is for us to place our hearts and minds into a position where we are happy with ourselves and also with others.

Messages from the Heart

"Be of good cheer," said the blind man, "and I will show you the way. Even though I cannot see, I have the knowledge to guide you in all aspects of your spiritual path."

If we listen to our hearts, the answers will come from within, and it is up to every one of us to trust what we are given, because it's not our conscious minds that are working but the words that are communicated by our guides or helpers.

Throughout the process of linking with Spirit we never know who will come to us until they do. Even then we may not know them. It is a learning path for each one of us, and we do not choose the information or the message that is provided.

Every message that is given to someone holds a purpose and is especially for that person so that he or she can learn from any negative or unkind actions that were done in a moment of indiscretion. It is, after all, a learning curve that will benefit everyone.

Sometimes we strive to understand the message, but we find it difficult to comprehend. This can be due to the way the information is delivered, which may be symbolic or may use an alternative method to get the point across. The point here is to understand that all messages can be given in different guises.

After all, we like a message that makes a positive connection from our loved ones.

The Beauty of the Mind

In the land of the living, we mature from a young child into a teenager and eventually into an adult. Along the way we have the choice to learn about everyday life and can take up a skill or a trade in engineering, commercial enterprises, banking or the like, or we may choose to become a lawyer, scientist, writer, musician, actor, artist, or singer.

But not everybody wants to aspire to a profession that is part of the fabric of our society. Some prefer to lead a more mundane way of life that is less complicated and less time-orientated. They allow the rigours of life to pass them by, which leads to less stress and a carefree approach, where they can take in what nature has to offer – the colours, the countryside, the views, and, above all, the beauty of our planet.

In all of this we have the ability to dream of the things that affect our lives. Some are inspirational, some are creative, and some are family-orientated and are a memory link from our earlier upbringing that gave us joy and pleasure.

The psychologist will say that dreams come from our subconscious mind that retains those memory links within our brain. They are stored as we grow up and are meant to activate the necessary information for us individually to move forward and gain an insight into ourselves.

But in essence, are we listening to our inner self, the voice that talks quietly to us in different disguises and the one who is always there for us?

Drinking from the Well

The font of all knowledge is within us, and as we progress, we need to draw upon it. Sometimes we are inspired by the thoughts that come into our heads, the thoughts that produce a plan or a project or that stir up a creativity to which are eyes are opened so that we may move forward.

Enlightenment is the fulfilment of the aims and ambitions that we have endeavoured to persevere with until the point of completion.

To say we are alike in forming our ideas is not entirely true, because we each have our own slant on how we perceive things. These initial thoughts formulate a basis week upon week – a foundation that can be administered for all to use, whether it is for practical or for spiritual guidance. When working as an individual or with a group, application and dedication are paramount to attain the desired goals for everyone. This can only be achieved by the willingness and cooperation of all those involved to reach a satisfactory conclusion.

In short, we open our minds to allow our guides to come close and speak the words necessary to provide comfort and solace.

The Brotherhood of Man

The brotherhood of man was devised to atone for our progress in all spiritual matters over many years from creation to the present time. Suffice it to say that man has aspired to reach the ultimate goal required to communicate at the highest level between souls in the etheric plains and those of us on the earth plains. In order to achieve the ultimate communication, we need to be dedicated, disciplined, and trusting in our guides, angels, and archangels. In everything we do, we always have somebody with us, who is always there for us, a protector, counsellor, and guide whom we may talk to. Sometimes decisions have to be made that cause us to contemplate the whys and wherefores that make up our free will. Once we have made a decision, the path forward is much clearer, and we move with confidence towards our objective. Throughout our lives, we have lived according to what we have felt was right or wrong, believing that it was our own decision, until we arrive at the point when we realise that it's not just us who make the decisions but it's also the one who is always with us.

The Twelve Chakras

As we all know, we are currently going through a transition in our spiritual life which involves changes within the structure of our chakras.

The chakra system has grown from seven to twelve chakras. The seven original chakras as we know them remain the same, and the additional five chakras are the platforms to enable us to reach our higher selves. Some of these five new chakras work with existing chakras, such as the heart and mind.

In essence, you have to visualise the platforms above your crown; each one is of a different ray that changes when joining with another chakra in colour.

The emphasis on these five chakras is to raise our awareness and allow us to work with our higher selves and also to connect with our ascended masters and for new guides to come into our lives. The process of working with these new guides will not daunt us but will be a continuation to improve our knowledge of working with ascended masters.

The path that we follow will always be one of progress, which will aid our spiritual advancement to a greater level of understanding, love and contentment.

Throughout our lives, we have felt that we were in charge of our destiny, but whatever went before us is changing to a more meaningful path that our ego has no control over. Our aim therefore is to walk in the light, heal those that are afflicted, help a friend, and nurture the young.

The Communicator

Together we will work together, you as the communicator and I as the vessel by which transmissions of information, philosophy, and messages are given.

This is a situation whereby the giver passes the messages to the receiver, who then delivers the message to the intended person. In short, the communicator relays a message that will benefit the person or one that they may not wish to hear. In effect, it's not the message the person wants to hear but one that is to the person's best interest.

Sometimes we make decisions that we feel are right, but after a while we discover that we should have made a different decision. Not everybody gets the decision right first time. So we learn from this and know what to do next time. Sometimes our ego gets in the way, because we are human. This inevitability comes at a cost and is one we learn from quickly.

The answer comes from within and is the one we should listen to. If you think about it, you lose the communicator's message when you should be listening to your inner ear.

All is not lost, however. By talking to your communicator you can recover from any errors that you have made and move forward with confidence.

Guardian Angel

As your guardian angel, I am here to guide you and protect you along your chosen path, as long as you listen to your intuition.

We work together as one whatever circumstances may occur. In life on the earth plains you live according to your beliefs, whilst my role as your guardian is to guide you in your spiritual connections so that the two worlds share as one.

It is with your belief that we are able to work together by using your human frame as the vessel. By placing your trust in me, you will have achieved your spiritual self.

Always have faith in your guardian angel that has been with you since your birth. Your guardian angel is your protector and walks with you throughout your life. You may speak with your guardian angel at any time for guidance, support, and reassurance, to alleviate any fears that you may have.

Bear in mind that your conscious decisions are made only by you. This is called free will. Whatever decision you make will be a learning curve as to whether you made the correct decision or not.

As we connect, you are allowing me, your guardian angel, to transfer my words through your body into the written form. You with your conscious mind have stood aside by placing your trust in me.

Crystals

Crystals have been used as far as time can be remembered. These crystals are formed within the earth and come in all forms, with different colours and healing properties for use when treating physical, spiritual, and emotional ailments.

The most well-known crystals are the ones used in the temples of Atlantis and other places throughout the world, such as inside mountains, the strength of which no man can measure in terms of power.

Throughout man's time on earth, crystals have been used for alignment between certain points between the earth and the planets within our universe, along with lay lines from an earlier generation between existing sites that are well known around the country and other parts of the world. Temples were constructed and laid out in a specific location that had an alignment with another temple and the sun. For example, Stonehenge on midsummer solstice has an alignment with the sun.

Our most common use for crystals today is for healing purposes to channel the energy from the crystal to an individual person to aid recovery of an ailment. Several crystals can be aligned along a person's body to balance a person's chakra system when there is an imbalance or when a chakra is blocked and needs realignment.

Crystals have been around for centuries and are used by many different nations. Even today people wear them or carry one in a purse or in their pocket, because when you have one, it will aid your physical or spiritual life.

Upliftment

Throughout our lives there are periods of upliftment, which make us feel good, happy, and full of joy. Above all there is a feeling of satisfaction.

This may have come about by inspiration during our work, listening to music, or just relaxing. It is during these quiet times that thoughts and words come into our head. Some of them may inspire us to create a work of art, write a piece of music, or start a novel. One could say that we have had a brain wave, but we know better: these inspirations are planted in our minds that give us the kick start to achieve these goals.

Other situations that create upliftment occur in sport. Whether you are an individual or a team player, it just takes one person to raise his or her game that will give him or her advantage over the other competitors. Such is the joy amongst the team, because they are part of the team, and success is celebrated between them.

These moments also occur in an educational setting. Students sit exams to achieve higher grades in different subjects, to gain a diploma, or to obtain a degree in their chosen subject. In all cases students have to study steadfastly and spend many hours pouring over books, case studies, and old exam papers to gain the honours they desperately need.

The euphoria that erupts on attaining their desired result is one of relief, joy, and upliftment for all to see.

Progress of a Medium

During our progress of enlightenment, we learn from our guides who teach us different aspects on our spiritual path.

These guides can be angels or archangels from a different dimension according to how we are developing. In the beginning we learn the basics and then progress to another guide who will teach us something else that will move us forward.

It is not a race to become a medium but a gradual and patient progression. Sometimes we feel that the pace is too slow, but Spirit controls our development and only allows us to move upwards to another level when they think we are ready.

To enhance our progress, we need to meditate on a regular basis in order to project ourselves into the spiritual connection. This can be achieved within your own home or by being part of a circle or closed circle led by an experienced medium.

The aim being is to take you on a journey by visualising what you see in your third eye along the path that you are taken. You will see people, gardens, landscapes, colours, rivers, mountains, buildings and trees. You may meet a guide from a higher dimension, who will give you a proverb for you to think about. You may also see a relative of yours from the spirit world, who wants to give you reassurance that the work you are doing will be rewarded in heaven.

Love Divine

Love, they say, is what makes the world go round. It's what everyone thrives on. Whether it is for a wife, husband, partner, child, friend, or an animal, these are all essential to forming the bond that holds you together.

In everyday life we look for and nurture this love, because it is precious to us. It's like water; we cannot exist without it – except that love is what we feel, and we need to share that love with another to fulfil the union.

Across the centuries many stories have been written about couples who declared their love for one another, some being high profile and others ordinary people. Love can test us in many ways, some good and some bad. Love is blind, as the saying goes, because we cannot see beyond love, and this can be painful at times.

It is not always smooth sailing in a relationship, so there has to be mutual cooperation to overcome difficulties that may arise. This can only strengthen the bond between two people.

There can also be many joyous times to be had with a wife, husband, partner, child, or friend when sharing quality time together, such as birthdays, anniversaries, weddings, and baptisms or when attending a function like a concert, dancing, eating out, the theatre, or an orchestral recital. There are many ways to complement a loving partnership.

But most of all, our spiritual life transcends not only our human life but also our family and friends, who have passed to the spiritual world, which we can share due to the love of God.

Reincarnation of the Spirit

Many years ago before the arrival of Jesus, the people believed in Spirit and therefore communicated with Spirit. It did not matter if you were in Egypt, Greece, Jordan, Syria, or Mesopotamian; the belief was strong in knowing that our loved ones lived on within the spirit world.

There are so many souls in Spirit now, even allowing for those who have returned from a past life several times, because of the lessons one needs to learn from past mistakes here on the earth plains. It is an option that one can return to earth in order to correct any misdemeanours one may have had carried out in a previous life. We look upon this as karma. Each person can return up to seven times in order to fulfil their contract with God.

Once you have completed your lives on earth, you will have the opportunity to lead a different life in another form, which is unlike anything here on the earth plains. You will come across people in another galaxy who will communicate in a different way, not by speaking but by thought processes, transferring your thoughts to another person and vice versa.

After all, mediums are already doing this when they receive messages from the spirit world, so whatever galaxy you end up in, you will have no fear, because Spirit is always with you.

Our Friends

What we want most in life besides our partners and lovers are friends who are there for us when we need them most. It's not just when we are celebrating a happy occasion; it's also when we are sad and feeling down. We need that upliftment to help us feel confident and raise our spirits out of the gloom.

Friends can also be an inspiration in our everyday life, even when they are not with us in person, such as when we communicate by telephone, email, Facebook, or the internet.

Your friendships may have started from a young age, perhaps when you were at school together. These bonds that are formed between us are strong in the knowledge that we have gained a friend for life.

Our personalities blend with one another. We like the same things, we share our thoughts, and we go to events together. There is so much satisfaction in being a friend to someone. Age makes no difference in knowing that they are there for you with a smile, a helping hand, kind words, or just reassurance that you are not alone. The time spent together can mean so much, and your heart feels so much lighter.

Our dearest friends are not always the ones that we can see but the ones we cannot see, for they have passed before their time. But they never leave us. They are always in our hearts and minds, wherever we may be.

The greatest friends can be found in the universe. They surround us with love and support, such as the angels and archangels who watch over us throughout our lives.

The Colour Yellow

The colours of the spectrum are spectacular in their display, each one vivid in texture and bloom. To all of us, a particular colour is a favourite and resonates with us in our dress sense, our home décor, and the colour of our car.

Colours are beneficial in other ways. In our spiritual work, when we refer to our chakras, each one is a part of our being, and at times a specific colour is needed to redress our spiritual balance for the good of our health, mind, and body.

The colour yellow denotes the engine of our body and is the driving force to control the function of our body, linking all systems within as one operating, programmed system.

Yellow is a delicate pastel colour that brings gentleness, serene and regal provenance that is inspiring to all who love it.

A Pink Bubble

In our younger years we recall playing with bubbles. We would blow them and watch them float away, as if drifting in time and space. We were mesmerised by the colour and sizes of the bubbles.

We were also fascinated by the presence of a bubble. How could it float along without any form of power and with nothing inside except air or just a vacuum.

When we think of ourselves inside a bubble, we feel as if we are free-floating along in space with no thought of time or where we are going.

But now imagine a pink bubble filled with love, a bubble that you can send to someone to help them overcome any disagreement, misunderstanding, or misdemeanour that has occurred between you.

The essence of sending love is a form of healing for both of you. Not only will it make you feel good about yourself; it will also help the other person to acknowledge that love.

We do not need to hold a grudge, tell a lie, and be uncharitable to another person, when all we need to do is to give love with feeling and understanding.

Autumn Leaves

The autumn leaves are falling, and the nights are getting colder. We need that extra layer of clothing, that thicker duvet or additional blanket to keep us snug and safe. The temperature takes on the chill factor, and the winds play havoc with the trees, the garden fencing, and anything that is not properly secured.

It is the time also to build up our reserve stores so that our energy is not depleted for the coming winter ahead. Dig out the old recipes of hot stews, shepherd's pies, and meat dishes to sustain us and keep out the cold.

You must treat your body as a temple and fill it with good things that nurture the body and mind, so that energy is maintained during the course of the winter.

It is a time for recharging the engine of the body and for fortifying the soul with love and kindness to those who are elderly, frail, disabled, and not able to cope with everyday life.

Our compassion comes to the fore when we are required to help the afflicted and the infirm. There is a feeling within us that lights up when we have satisfied our physical and spiritual obligations to those that need them most.

The deliverance comes from the heart and good intent to help one another.

Grandparents

The joys of becoming a grandparent fill us with love and gratitude upon the birth of any grandchild. You are brought into this world to fulfil life's journey from the womb of your mother to many years of adventure throughout your life here on earth as long as it may take you.

As you grow from a baby, you are fed and watered, loved and doted upon every minute of the day. Your family constantly tends to your needs with food to help you grow and with games to play with and amuse you.

Your education is also provided to help you gain knowledge and learning in several subjects that will enhance your opportunities to gain the academic certificates that you strives for.

So too will the path towards your working life become more evident in the things that you are attracted to. You may wish to work with your hands, to create a product, become a farmer, fisherman, or factory worker, or you may wish to use your brain in a legal, actuarial, banking, insurance, managerial or sales role.

In any of these positions you are fulfilling your path to learn and achieve whatever heights you want to ascend to.

Throughout your journey you will have been supported by your family, including your grandparents, who will cherish your progress throughout your upbringing with love and support in everything you do.

A New-born Baby

We welcome a new-born baby onto the earth plains like a new-born lamb. It is so tender and fragile in its appearance, yet it is strong enough to give voice to say, "I am here at last."

Upon your arrival there is so much expectation from your loved ones and joy that you are perfectly formed and everything is in the correct position. Little did we know that such a bundle of joy should overwhelm us and bring so much happiness!

Now there is another one to love and cherish, to watch and grow in stature from those first unsteady steps, all part of the progress of a child in its early years.

The bond that grows between the child and its parents is strong and caring; likewise the child is dependent on its parents to be there for it at such a young age.

Our lives are interwoven with each other in all aspects, such as the first time the child speaks one word or one name to a very proud parent.

In those early years the child learns to eat, sleep, play, walk, and talk. It is all part of a learning curve to become an individual who can make his or her mark in life and fulfil his or her ambitions.

My Archangel

Our lives are filled with so many good things. We feel ecstatic when we are filled with joy, happiness, love, and excitement. The world feels like a wonderful place to be.

We share so many of these things with our family and loved ones on a day-to-day basis, ensuring the bonds are strong. We strive to strengthen our relationships, always projecting them forward in a positive manner to achieve their goals and status in life.

We need to balance our lives with the material and spiritual aspects of what we need to live a fulfilled and happy life. There may be stumbling blocks along the way that are difficult to overcome. Sometimes we need to make a decision, either to take the path to the left or to the right. We won't know the correct path until we have taken the one we feel is from our inner self. Sometimes we need to discuss and share these decisions to come to a satisfactory conclusion.

You know the old saying that two heads are better than one. This is when you trust your archangel to work with you and gain the inspiration that you need.

The culmination of working together to a satisfactory conclusion is rewarding in itself. Working with your Archangel is a joy, knowing many more times spent together will bring forth success.

Dreams

Our dreams and aspirations are given to us mostly when we are asleep. Sometimes they are compelling and vivid in their formation and almost real.

We ponder on our dreams to try and make sense of what we are seeing. Some stretch our imagination, inspire us, and fill us with confidence in a positive manner to achieve our dreams.

Not everyone can remember the dreams that they have had, but they will be relayed to us again to show us how we should move forward.

A dream is like a journey that has been planted in our mind, in which we can travel to anywhere in our world or another galaxy. There are no limits within our dreams, such as colours, shapes and sizes, textures, materials, buildings, ships, aircraft, motor cars, buses, trains, landscapes, mountains, rivers, the sea, people, animals, and many of the other things that we can see.

The truth is that we can choose to believe in our dreams or not. It is a choice of free will that gives us an option to make our dreams come true or to cast them aside. Either way you choose, always remember it could be your guide or archangel who has planted this dream inside your head to show you that anything is possible. All you have to do is make that dream come true.

One Small Step

Take a small step at a time, and doors will open before you that were previously closed, allowing you to progress without fear and trepidation.

People that held back will now come forward to put you at your ease, mindful of what went before you and them. The laughter returns within you that did not shine in isolation; although you strived to engage in mutual topics, the repartee did not flow.

We wondered what the problem was. The response was slow, somewhat half-hearted, as if there was a lack of commitment. Time seemed to be immaterial in forming decisions that lacked content and clarity.

To be at one with another, everything needs to flow on a material and spiritual level in order to strike the right balance, in which both of you seek to appease the other, making sure the outcome is right for both of you.

The joy of seeing the light at the end of a dark tunnel is satisfaction in itself. Having been through a period of denial and self-doubt, the elation is there for all to see.

We have come full circle to a point of realisation that any fears that we may have had are now unfounded and our path forward is free from obstacles.

Christmas

As we move forward to Christmas for the celebration of Jesus's birth with joy and with peace to all upon the earth, we should cast aside the conflict of war and come together in peace and reconciliation for the good of all peoples. We should have learnt by know that war is not the answer to the problems that some countries differ about.

Many years have passed since the coming of Jesus. We have progressed on our life paths, and we have learned from the mistakes we have made on our journey the lessons of life.

As we come nearer to the day of the Christmas festival, let us remind ourselves of the spiritual meaning of this event.

The coming began in a lowly stable with shepherds, kings and animals to mark Jesus's arrival. There were no comfortable surroundings here, just the basic necessities when entering a new life.

You come into this world with nothing, and you go out with nothing except the knowledge you have gained whilst being on the earth.

Your return to the spiritual universe will be met with joy in abundance. Meeting with your loved ones again will be the culmination of your life's journey. Should you have worked upon your spiritual path whilst you were on earth, you will have fulfilled your life's purpose, and to this end you will have followed in Jesus's path.

A Child Is Born

The love we have for our family, parents, grandparents, siblings, children, and grandchildren can only be measured in the emotions that we feel for one another.

An event such as the birth of a new baby can bring so much joy to all concerned. During the Christmas period, we celebrate the birth of Jesus, and the birth of any other child around this time is also a special occasion.

A new life is brought into this world of ours with so many expectations on the child and also on ourselves. We want the best possible start for the child, and we will make every effort to ensure that this will happen.

Every child that comes to our earth plains is a gift from the spiritual world to grow, learn, follow the paths of righteousness, and achieve his or her aims and obligations in life.

Every parent in this situation for the first time will be apprehensive of his or her role and expectations in bringing up a child.

The one thing for sure will be the love that transcends from the parents to their child, in glowing admiration and wonder, and the child will return that love with mutual spontaneity.

We protect our children during those early stages, and later on as they grow in stature, with security in mind we take every precaution to keep them safe from harm, to lead a happy life that is rewarding and fulfilling for all members of our family.

Love is the strongest emotion that comes from the heart, and with it come the ties that bind us together as a family.

Our Faith

Through the many realms within the worlds, we each have a faith in ourselves and a following which is spiritual and one that we believe in.

Over the centuries, churches have been built in many different countries that reflected their way of living and spiritual paths, each one reflecting on them was a form of worship in their own tongues, whether it was Christian, Roman Catholic, Greek Orthodox, Hindu, Muslim, or religions of the New World.

In each case everyone prayed to their God in their own way, believing theirs was the right way to lead a righteous life in which they would have peace and contentment.

However not all were peaceful. Wars broke out that divided nations and peoples, to the point where each person turned to his or her god for salvation.

Some people were ostracised for their beliefs, but the majority had the conviction to believe in their faith and carried on praying anyway. Those that did have the faith were restored in humanity, humbleness, and humour, to the point that they felt good about themselves, lending a hand where necessary. Healing the sick, bereaved, friends and neighbours is all part of loving God and being at peace with one's self.

Whatever church or religion you belong to, know in your heart that there is only one true God.

A Place for Us

There is a place for us on the earth plains that resonates with our souls in ways that we cannot explain. It can sometimes be the beauty that we are surrounded with, the stillness in a remote place that enables us to think clearly and with clarity to such an extent that everything becomes very clear and precise.

The mind creates and perceives ideas and thoughts to enhance the magic of words in our spiritual being. To learn is to know that knowledge is beneficial to us all. The fountain of all knowledge provides us with the bricks to form our working lives to a level of intellect that we thought was not possible.

Our path may lie in several directions, and we may not know for sure which one to take, but over time and through thought processes we come to a conclusion which is the right one. In all aspects of our journey we follow the path that seems right for us without question, not knowing whether or not there are pitfalls, for from this uncertainty we will learn in more ways than you can think of.

Accepting our callings is to believe in ourselves and those around us who support us, for our paths are laid out before us and our places secured.

The Spiritual Connection

The understanding between you and your spirit guides allows you to connect words of wisdom so that you may write them down. Your conscious mind has to step aside in order for you to receive the dialogue. The truth is what you hear, and this is what you need to impart to others.

The reality comes to the fore if your evidence about the communicator passes onto you the details of a relative, a loved one, a friend, or someone else that you do not yourself know when giving a demonstration.

The evidence does not always make sense when you are giving information to another being. The messenger may have come from a generation that you did not meet or know especially if you were a young child or you were adopted or separated from your family.

To all of us, the connection is very important for our well-being, knowing that there is always love, no matter how far apart we may be in time and distance. The reality is that our loved ones are never far from us, and we should place our trust in them to guide us on our paths.

It can be of great comfort to a medium to channel messages that are well received and to know that he or she is maintaining that bond with Spirit.

The Colour Green

Our land is plentiful in colour for most of the year; we have a variety which creates a wonderful show during the spring and summer and even into the autumn. The one colour that stands out is the colour green, for it has so many shades that sometimes we do not see them, as if they are being disguised by more attractive colours around.

The colour is evident in all sorts of plants, trees, shrubs, grasses, vegetables, and fruits. All these things grow upon the earth for our health and well-being to nurture us in the beauty that surrounds us every day of our lives.

If we did not have the colour green, we would not have the benefit of healthy food. By walking in beautiful hills and landscapes in many parts of the planet, we absorb the scenery before us.

In some cases it is said that we can be green with envy at someone else's success or achievement.

Green issues abound in our everyday lives, particularly how we recycle our waste and packaging to sustain our planet from being contaminated. This is our way of preserving nature, our habitats, trees, shrubs, plants, and anything green within our landscapes.

The spiritual world is also abundant in the colour green, for it comes from the heart with love to all that seek it.

It is up to every one of us to remember that love is the bond that unites us together.

The Colour Purple

Is there any colour that stands out more than the colour purple, with its richness and depth of feeling that are transmitted to everyone that embraces it?

We look upon the colour purple as our spiritual connection that brings us closer to God and our heavenly beings. The divine connection that links us with our family and friends to make us feel comfortable in ourselves and the love that surrounds us every day are constant reminders that bond us together as families irrespective of the problems of the modern world.

The colours of the universe are infinitely spectacular. And they glow with such intensity that it's no surprise to us that these colours are real. Such is the beauty you see in the assorted flowers in your garden, the parks, stately homes, exhibitions, flower shows, and wild flowers.

Each one of us has a favourite colour that resonates within us and is quite obvious in our fashion tastes. The beauty of colour we demonstrate in our artwork, flower arranging, and home decorations are some of the ways we project our skills as individuals.

There is one colour that we have focused upon from an early age, that stays with us throughout our adult lives, and that never leaves us. Some people regard this special colour as lucky to them, and it complements their aura.

Whatever colour you have chosen is meant for you and will shine upon you with radiance.

Memories

For those of you that have had happy memories, this is a blessing upon you, for not everyone can say that they have such memories.

Throughout our lives there have been moments to treasure from an early age until the present day. Most of these have occurred at special times – for example, coming of age, learning to drive and passing the test, attaining those all-important grades at school, progressing to university and gaining a degree, your first trip abroad, or obtaining a job that you desired that started you off onto the ladder of success. They might have been when you became engaged to someone that you love and eventually got married. Perhaps it was your first house together, your first child, their first birthday, or their first Christmas. These are all special times that will remain in your heart for a long time.

Through the passage of time, we retrieve these moments to remind us of those joyous times we had; they meant a lot to us at the time they happened. Probably these events would have been recorded in photo albums or on video or downloaded onto CDs or DVDs so that we may capture those special moments and relive these moments from the past that are stored away in our brains.

Most of us need to reflect upon those events that occurred at a time when change was evident in our lives. We can look back with admiration at our own progress and the progress of our families.

The place where we all want to be is one of progress, success, and belief in knowing that the faith that we have followed will lead us to our loved ones in the Promised Land.

Inspiration

In each and every one of us there is scope for inspiration, to enable us to create things in our lives – maybe an artistic impression, composing a musical score, playing an instrument, or writing a novel, an autobiography, or a poem. In any case you will be led by the thought process within your mind, as if what you seek is already being transformed into painting, playing, or writing your desired subject. Time is immaterial when creating a work of art, a musical symphony or a play.

During our lifetime the pace seems so frenetic that we barely have time to think, due to the pressures of work in our daily lives. But when we stop and ponder in our own isolation, we begin to connect. We form ideas to produce a plan, to find a way to build something, or to see a way around an obstacle.

Sometimes we seek inspiration in all forms of colours, shapes, figures, words, or music – anything that can lift us to a level that makes us feel that anything is obtainable.

A good example is the Olympics. A typical scenario involves athletes being inspired by the crowd in our own country that raises their performances to record levels. The exhilaration everyone feels at this time is testament to the commitment, fitness, and discipline of the athletes. Inspiration can teach us many things in achieving our own aims.

Springtime

The flowers in springtime bring forth so much freshness into our daily lives. Their variety and colour is the beginning of the growing season. The pick-me-up is what we need after the winter months. It rejuvenates us and moves us on with a spring in our step, ever mindful that the spring is a wonderful time of the year.

The new lambs are around, the birds are singing, the hedgerows and the trees are beginning to show buds and leaves, the daylight hours are drawing out, and the temperature is getting warmer.

In ourselves we feel brighter and happier in the knowledge that the year is unfolding before us. The sun adds that extra sparkle to us and provides the additional energy that we need and feel.

Energy is what our bodies need in order to function properly. The food that we require is varied and consists of nutrients, vitamins, and proteins. All these things help us to sustain our daily lives; each item of our intake supplements the workings of our organs, blood flow, bone density, muscles, and brain tissue to the point where we realise that our bodies need all of these items to exist as a human being, ever mindful that we are complex beings of the universe in mind, body, and soul.

Love

Love is all around us in our daily lives. There are so many ways to see love that we do not always see or feel it.

Love can be with a friend, a partner, a wife, a husband, children, parents, siblings, or other family members. Sometimes this love can be taken for granted, because the ones that matter have our best interests at heart. They are there for us in everything we do.

Love needs to be reciprocated between two people to maintain the bond that has been created in order to fulfil the union.

To show love is to demonstrate your affection to the person you care about. A gift to a loved one does not need to be extravagant or expensive. A gift should come from the heart and have a personable touch with words of feeling.

What is said between lovers, man and wife, or partners needs to be said with sensitivity, compassion, and caring. We need to share things with family, relatives, and our closest friends.

Laughter is one attribute which should be maintained throughout any relationship. It's what keeps us happy and allows us to smile. Trust needs to be the common factor with each other, as it enables growth on both sides and eliminates the thought of fear.

Other kinds of love are important too. For example, love between humans and their pets, such as a dog, cat, budgie, horse, gerbil, or rabbit, can be a bond formed in early childhood that carries on for some years. We never forget our pets that have passed over, and our memories bring them back from time to time.

Our greatest love is not here on the earth plains, but for those who sacrificed so much for us when they were here with us, our love remains constant with them for evermore.

Planet Earth

The lives of people are many and varied. Across the continents there are many who speak different languages that have been handed down over the centuries. Even before the coming of Jesus, many spoke in different dialects depending on the country they lived in. This is not unusual, because people crossed over from one country to another with the aim of conquering the inhabitants and installing their own language upon the home nation.

This has been borne out by the Romans, Greeks, Turks, Vikings, Saxons, Normans, and Celts, all of whom left their mark in some way, including architecture, art, music, civil engineering, medicine, and religion.

Over the years, integration has not always been to our liking, but progress has inevitably run its course to where we are today. We have learnt to accept these invaders from time to time, and all the while we have learnt many things from them, which have been to our advantage in schools and colleges, such as languages, history, geography, engineering, and art.

We have come a long way on the road over the centuries. Looking back, progress has been made in all areas at a substantial level, and one wonders what can be achieved in the future and at what cost to the planet earth.

Too many people progress is a fine thing, but we need to look at how we live, the part we play in life, and what we need to balance the life of our planet in order to survive.

If we do not place our faith and trust in God, we will only have ourselves to blame. We need to believe in ourselves, and our faith will be rewarded.

Your Grandmother

This message is full of love from your dearest one in Spirit. It's been a long time since I passed, and you were a little girl, so you may not remember much of me. Nevertheless, I adored you as a child. I am your grandmother. As I watched you growing up, you made me feel so proud. You have done well at school and also in your working life.

Your dedication and devotion in everything that you have done have stood you in great stead.

The one thing that you miss is your loved ones in Spirit. We know that many of us have been reassured that the soul lives on in the spirit world and is always with us, even though we don't always realise it. You may think you see somebody pass by the window or you might see a small coloured light when the lights are switched off and you are just lying there in your bed. This is the signal that a relative or loved one is very close. You can be reassured that they come around you and want to be near you.

This is the time to feel contented and comforted, because you accept that your loved ones live on in the spirit world.

Our lives are evolving so that we feel part of the two worlds. Our journey on the earth plains is relatively short, but the time we spend in the spirit world cannot be measured, because there is no time over there. You can be anywhere you want in a split second. Travel is no problem, and should you ask for them to be near you, they will.

Those that pass to Spirit are going home. Your time upon the earth is a journey to learn a lesson about yourself.

The Light

The light is always with us wherever we are. It is our protection, along with our guardian angel, and we work with the light to enhance our spiritual progress in all areas, such as a medium, psychic artist, spiritual writer, or healer.

In all cases, the spiritual connection is made purely with the light in mind, body, and soul, together with our guides, communicators, and guardian angels.

The link between men and women enables us as humans to make the connection with Spirit. The one thing that is required from us is the desire to make it happen. We do not operate from our conscious minds, but through a meditative state we are able to connect with the light.

Light comes in all colours of the rainbow. Each colour signals a healing property that is relevant to a particular part of our bodies that requires a balance both physically and spiritually.

The work we carry out with our guides, communicators, and archangels is a partnership where both work together to channel the information and the messages of love and support to those who need it most.

To make this happen, we are required to have faith and trust in what we believe in and know that our loved ones are never very far away.

The Soul

We are grateful for the support and guidance that our souls have afforded us on our spiritual journey. Our path is a continual one that takes us to the spiritual horizons in our third eye.

We never know where we are being led. Such is the beauty of our astral travel that allows us to look down from the skies and observe the earth below in all its majesty.

We can look back in time to a previous life that taught us something about existing in a harsher or difficult times many years ago. We did manage somehow with the help of our guides and helpers, although we may not have recognised them at the time.

For us, seeing is a normal function that takes little effort on our part, but to see spiritually is another matter that requires a meditative state for the third eye to open.

To see colours, people, places, and loved ones in Spirit is a joy that helps us understand that there is more to life than just living on the earth plains.

How many times have we been here? We cannot remember those previous lives, because they have been erased. When we leave the earth plains, only our souls remain in the transition to the spirit world, where we meet up again with our loved ones.

Dream Travel

My dreams are always filled with the continuous travel through time and space as we embark with our guides and family members to all corners of the earth. Astral travel allows us to float within our minds to regions of life in the past, or it can show us spectacular views throughout the universe that we would not normally see.

Dreams can also be a reminder of someone or something that was special to us in our lives.

We may also have a recurring dream that is meant to teach us something about ourselves so that we may learn about our path here on earth.

In each case, the emphasis is upon our spiritual selves. We can improve our ways or rely on our spiritual guides. This will enable us to progress and reach a higher level so that we can connect with the true light.

Our ultimate goal is to work with our ascended masters to obtain the purest of light in mind, body, and spirit. To achieve this, we need to place our trust in God and become disciplined in carrying out our spiritual work.

To believe is to have faith in ourselves and those that went before us, for they are there whenever we need them to guide us on our way. As long as you have faith within your heart, they will never let you down. The truth is always spoken.

The Elements

The elements of the earth have been a part of us for thousands of years. There are four main elements: air, earth, fire, and water. Each of them has been generated as a part of our existence, and each is vital in the make-up of the earth.

The air that we breathe enables us to function as human beings existing upon the earth. We cannot live without air. It is our lifeline.

THE BRETHREN SPIRIT

Earth forms the foundation for all living things to grow, and it is also part of our lives, for it creates the carbon dioxide we need in the air, and it is required in our blood cells to maintain our physical condition and the functions of the heart.

Fire is an element that is used to create heat for the purposes of cooking our food. It is also used to heat our homes, to boil water for creating steam to drive a pump or a train. Fire can be formed from natural causes that ravage and destroy woodland, homes, and other areas.

Water is the element we need to drink in order to survive. It is our lifesaver, and without it we would not exist. Water is also required for our planet – the trees, shrubs, flowers, vegetables, and animals of all species. The sea covers a vast area of the planet; this allows many creatures to live and multiply and is also a source of food for us all.

Wood is used in many other ways, such as in the construction of our homes. Tools were first made from wood, and wood furniture has long been used to make us comfortable. For centuries, ships have been made from wood, and wooden boats are still used for sailing.

The four elements were created millions of years ago. Man has used them in order to survive, and we will still do so as long as we place our trust in God.

Beings of Light

We are all beings of light. We have a combination of physical and spiritual abilities within our make-up. To us we are a complicated formula, consisting of bodies with bones, muscles, internal organs, blood, a brain, nerves, and the ability to think for ourselves. To combine all these things is a work of genius and wonder.

Functioning as human beings is all part of the growth of our bodies and our ability to learn about life, ourselves, and what we think we want from an early age.

Throughout our lives we make conscious decisions that we feel are right, only to find that circumstances or events change our decisions and have a bearing on which way we should turn or go next. Conscious decisions are not always the correct ones. They can lead to mistakes as we travel along our paths in life. These mistakes are termed as learning curves. Although painful at times, they actually turn out to our advantage.

We begin to listen to the thoughts that are planted in our minds as if someone is encouraging us to move forward and not backwards, as this can have a detrimental effect. To be guided by Spirit is, after all, the one true way to overcome any misgivings about your life up to now. Take the positive approach, and

THE BRETHREN SPIRIT

believe and trust in your intuition, because you are being guided.

The spiritual life is of great importance to each of us, because it is one half of the body and reflects through the brain the connection that exists. We are all light, and we come from light to prove that life is eternal upon the earth, as well as in the spiritual world.

The Flowers

The flowers of the earth grow in such profusion! They provide an array of colour in so many different varieties. We marvel at their formation. Size is important, because to us there is so much beauty in every different type of flower.

To the vast majority of us, growing flowers is a hobby that gives us a lot of pleasure in developing and creating a wonderful display in our own gardens. It is not the effort or the pain which drives us to establish a work of art through growing flowers in a display of sheer genius. Planting different colours of mixed plants or seeds can sometimes be a lottery, and other times you have to let nature take its course. The amount of time tending our gardens is not measured, only for us to admire the full display when all is in full bloom.

Flowers mean so much to us in our lives. We give them to friends, family, and loved ones for celebrations and to the bereaved in their hour of sorrow. There is so much meaning in giving flowers to someone else. Doing so can bring happiness, fulfilment, and joy at a birth, a birthday, an anniversary, or a wedding. It can also bring comfort at the loss of a loved one or a friend.

Most of all, flowers offer colour, formation, style, warmth, beauty, fragrance, and arrangement. We can admire them in the garden or display them in a flower arrangement that can light up a home, church, hall, or meeting place. The feeling that we get when we see them raises our senses and our admiration that the earth is a beautiful place to live in, wherever we are.

Life Eternal

Life eternal is the time that passes when one's soul lives in the spiritual world and in physical form upon the earth. We do not know exactly how many lives we have lived over the generations. Each time may have been in a different part of the world many years ago.

The reason we come back is to learn the lessons of life that we previously had not learnt, and to lead a better life in which we are more at peace with ourselves by adapting to the obstacles placed in our path.

Life is never easy, no matter whom you are, and we all need to learn from mistakes in our past. It's not about taking, but learning how to give, by giving, you are making yourself and the person you are giving to happy and full of good cheer so that you can lift his or her soul and bring a smile to his or her face.

It is not about material gain but more about spiritual gain, knowing that what you are doing is right for you and your loved ones. The satisfaction of seeing them in their rightful place is enough for anybody.

Your spiritual life can give pleasure in many ways. Being part of a church or a healing group, tutoring a circle, working as a medium, writing to channel words of wisdom, and psychic art all lead to a better life – a life we were meant to lead according to the contract we made before we came back to the earth.

Our existence in the spiritual realm is one where we also work together with others, such as family members, friends, guides, angels, and archangels, to help our loved ones wherever they may be.

Archangel Michael

This message is of the most importance to those that want to follow the path of the divine light. We are all Spirit, and even though we may not feel the same way while on the earth, we are indeed of one spirit in body and soul.

Those of you who work with spirit are fulfilling your purpose here on earth and for us in the spirit world; it is the culmination of working together as one for what we believe in.

The faith you have shown tells us of the beliefs you hold within yourselves and the love and respect you hold so dear for all mankind.

Every day you may feel that you have a mountain to climb, but this is not the case. It is a path of steady progress and dedication for everyone. Some of you are working at different levels, but do not think that you are lagging behind. This is not a race; we decide our own rate of progress on our journey.

Everyone must show patience in their work to attain the levels of working with divine masters. There are no short cuts when working with Spirit. Your guides, archangels, and masters decide upon your progress.

The joy you feel when your ability to connect and to receive a message is also felt by us in Spirit, along with your family and friends, in the knowledge that you are fulfilling your life's purpose.

Archangel Michael. You can be assured that should you call upon me, I will be at your side; it is our duty to safeguard all who work with us. There are many like me who work in specific areas. All of us are doing our jobs for the good of all men and women upon the earth. God bless you all!

Free Will

In life we have many lessons to learn. Some are to right the wrongs we have done in a previous life and some are to correct our mistakes during our current life.

We never know for sure if the decisions we have made are right or wrong until we commit ourselves. Even then it can take some time to unravel whether we have made the right choice or not.

In all cases, our decisions come from free will alone, and we may have pondered over this dilemma and turned it over several times in our minds.

To correct past decisions from a previous life, we have to look within ourselves. Sometimes we know about them from a recurring dream that we have not dealt with in a satisfactory way, and also from the thought of seeing someone or some place that we encountered before in a previous life.

This can be a constant reminder to encourage us to deal with an indecision that we keep putting off, and by reminding us, we know that we have to deal with it.

Throughout our lives we are faced with situations that on an everyday occurrence will require us as individuals to make the decision which we feel is right for us.

It is all about choices. Shall I or shan't I? Should I catch the bus to work or drive my car? (And on a sunny day I might ride my bicycle.) Too many options, you might say, but in the end it is all down to free will.

The Light Shines within Us

Within the realms of our minds, we have a vast expanse of knowledge. We do not know the capacity or the content within us. At various intervals we tap into our brains to recover a poem, a reading, or a prayer to remind us of the words that give us inspiration, enlightenment, and resolution to satisfy our thirst for learning.

It does not take much to engage with our guides or communicators in order to channel the words of love and healing from our loved ones in spirit. They can always link with you and address a situation where they can give you some tips on overcoming an obstacle that you cannot fathom out yourself. Your loved ones in spirit tend to come to you when they are most needed, but should this not be the case and if your life is working out as it should be, then they will leave you alone.

We cannot expect them to be with us every second of the day. We need time to ourselves, which is called "me time" when we can think things through and come up with the solutions that will fit into our everyday lives.

There is a light within us that shines with inner radiance and gives us a feeling of joy, healing, and compassion towards our family, friends, and loved ones who are special to us.

Our soul remains with us during our lifetime on the earth plains. It was designated to us in time immemorial. Souls can return to earth several times in different human forms and over a period of many years. They become old souls who are wise, learned, and true spirits in which the light within never goes out.

Understanding

In our hearts and minds we have the capacity to think, write, and communicate the words that enable us to understand one another on a physical and emotional level.

Sometimes what we say can be misunderstood, misconstrued, or misappropriated by the receiver, to the extent that the message was not interpreted in the way it was intended. For some people, this can come across as hurtful, deceitful, or painful, and it can cause the person to react in a negative or an aggressive manner that does not help anyone.

The remedy for this is to show love to that person to rectify any misgivings on either part. We have it in us to demonstrate our true feelings to the extent that love comes from the heart. In life we cannot always get everything right. Along the way we stumble on our path, putting right the wrongs we have done and asking for forgiveness.

Love does not come from the mind but from the heart, and this is the essence of our being – not something that was conjured up in our minds that we thought about. This feeling comes direct from the heart.

They say love is blind and is also beyond reason. That's because our conscious minds have not come into play, and the feeling of love overcomes us on a wave of emotion that beckons us to our destiny.

Spirituality

Spirituality is the primary and sole purpose of our existence. No matter how fulfilling our lives seem to be, our conscious minds forever want to strive for more materialistic things that have no spiritual value. We only do this to satisfy our own ego. Such a life has lost its purpose.

Spiritual growth can only be attained through the practice of universal love, which is unconditionally loving all life and treating all equally. The more love you hold, the higher you vibrate.

All life is equal, and no soul is greater than another. All are of one body and spirit. Spirituality is the essence and purpose of all souls. Everyone in your life can be your teacher, and all events in your life are lessons. If you do not learn from them, they will pose problems until you do finally learn. Walk through life with love.

Spiritual Direction and Meaning

We all need to feel that we have a spiritual meaning and purpose. By creating our spiritual direction and having goals and expectations, we are heading down a positive path that gives us something to hold onto every day.

Your work and dedication towards your goals will intensify your sense of spiritual meaning and purpose. Be true to your spiritual self, hold onto it, and live your life with love and compassion as best you can, evaluating the things in your life that hold the most importance – your family, your friends, and your job.

What it really comes down to is this: know what you want and know why you want it. Discover your talents and passions, and do not forget to use them every day.

You do not want expectations from others, so you should not expect things from others in return. Find your purpose in life, and love unconditionally.

Healing

The most precious gift of all has been handed down over thousands of years. Since the coming of Jesus Christ, healing has been carried out in several forms, such as spiritual, reiki, esoteric, Native American Shamanism, Sanskrit, acupuncture, crystal healing, and many others throughout the world.

I personally first became interested in spiritual healing after my parents had passed over into spirit. My mother and father had brought us up in the Christian way in the Church of England. We all went to church every Sunday with their three sons and one daughter, sometimes three times in one day (morning, Sunday school, and evensong). My sister and I were both in the choir, and I always felt at peace inside the church, it was a great place.

My spiritual interest deepened following the passing of my mother. I needed to know if my parents were in heaven, and so I attended a spiritual church and received a message from both of them. This was a great comfort to me, and I soon became interested in spiritual healing. A training course was about to start at a local Corinthians Church and Healing Association run by Rev Phil Phillips, a certified training healer. The course consisted of theoretical and practical study consisting of auric body system, the skeletal system, the muscular system, the nervous system, the circulatory system, the respiratory system, and listening skills. It was followed by exams and a trainee-healer practical application programme for one year under supervision.

What is important is that the healing is effective and that people from any belief may benefit from it. All people have the potential to be healers; healing is not of any one race or religion.

It must be realised that the potential to heal needs to be developed. Some of the qualities to assist the healer are love, compassion, tolerance, and genuine desire to heal.

In all cases, records are kept of all individuals receiving healing, with details of their health condition and the application of healing given by the healer.

The healer first enters into a meditation to form the link with a guide in order to channel the energy to the patient. The healer in most cases uses a couch for the patient to lie on. The purpose is for the patient to be in as relaxed a state as possible. Soft music or recorded sounds of nature are recommended, and a lighted candle is placed in the vicinity.

You ask the patient if they would like to be covered by a sheet or blanket to retain the energy. Once healing starts, you are guided by your guide to the area of the patient's body that needs healing channelled. It's always a good place to start around the head, where the patient will relax and will sometimes go into a sleep state due to the energy being channelled.

Under no circumstances should you try to heal someone who has a pacemaker fitted to their heart. This can be dangerous because of the energy that can affect the operation of the pacemaker.

The time spent healing depends on the person's condition. For some with a minor ailment, fifteen minutes is regarded as sufficient. In more painful conditions, thirty minutes would be of more benefit.

It is recommended that the healer gives the person a glass of water or a cup of tea after the healing has finished. This is a natural requirement that the body needs to settle. If the person is driving a car or other vehicle, he or she should wait at least fifteen minutes before leaving in order to ground him or herself.

Part 3

Guides, Past Life Regression, Trance Mediumship.

My Guide Karis

Karis is part of my soul group, mainly on a healing vibration and philosophy. Soon you may need to write down your dream experiences.

This leads to philosophy, spiritual direction to be put into the written word, later to be published.

Karis is of the blue-violet ray of the divine plan and is known as an angel of principality.

This group includes Silver Birch, Pioneers of Sportucles Cism, Conan Doyle, Oliver Lodge, and Confucius.

Karis's main work is "truth" communication from the third to the fifth dimension.

Illumination of Ray 14

Holding the reigns
In total control of your future aims,
Manifestation supreme of each and every dream,

It's yours for the asking.
Let your wishes be seen.
Guardians of the Fourteenth Ray are
The Pleiadean Beings of Light.

Past Life Regression by Delyse Bastista-Pedro

I saw you as a Roman soldier in Egypt; you wore breast armour over a dark red tunic with a navy blue cape, sometimes with a seal on the clasp.

Your whole life was the army, first, second, and last. You were strict but fair. While the men marched, you rode a horse, but sometimes you would march with the men all day to let them understand that you asked no man to do what you yourself could not do.

Your life was one of service and duty, responsibility for others.

You had no wife or sons, but many ladies came in and out of your life, but always it was duty first.

You were a fine strong dependable man who lived into what was old age – the late fifties. You chose to stay in Egypt and ended your days happily there.

You enjoyed watching new skills in horsemanship. You yourself had falcons that hunted and in later life two dogs. I do not recognise the breed, but they were good dogs.

This was an admirable life in which you learned much about life and men. You were interested in medicine for the men in your command and used much honey and cloves.

This was a busy life. You were quite stern and quiet, and a private man of inner strength.

Your name was Petros.

Past Life Regression by Jeff Powell (First Regression)

Breathing exercises and going into hypnosis. Entered through a dark wooden door arched in a wall, dressed in sandals and sackcloth. Walked on a sandy road to Damascus. Can see the walled city ahead in the distance. Carrying a bound manual. Male aged 27 years. Other people in the distance wearing similar clothes, some with coloured wraps and wearing head attire circular in shape with a coloured band.

The day was sunny with clear blue skies, and the air was warm.

My name was Luther with no surname.

Past Life Regression by Jeff Powell (Second Regression)

An event that occurred at Southmead Hospital in August 1983 was the birth of my second son. I was present at the birth. The procedure was very clear, and after he was born, he was put into an incubator to reduce jaundice. He recovered with much anxiety in three days, and we were able to take him home.

Dream Experiences and Outcomes

I was at home asleep in my bed around four o'clock to five o'clock in the morning, dreaming of being chased through a forest with pine trees all around. The person chasing me – I could not see his face, and when he got close, he grabbed my right arm. I resisted him by using all my strength and clenching my fist. I awoke with my heart pumping like mad, and gradually it died down, but there was a lot of activity in the heart area – gurgling and other noises that rumbled on for a few minutes. I then drifted off to sleep again.

My first thoughts when I had woken up were the actions in my dream. They made me think that spirit was diverting my attention whilst they were carrying out some adjustments to my heart and the force of moving my right arm was to pull me over onto my back.

That same day during the evening, I attended a development circle at Tony Blackmore's home with our regular circle friends. We spoke about my dream in the early hours, which I described to him.

Tony's reply was:

1. Fear ego based on the unknown. This is because of your spiritual path intention connecting with your conscious mind. Trees are faith, trust, and security.
2. Earthly situation is controlling you and not vice versa.
3. There is pressure of material conditions and others' expectations of you.
4. Now you are astral travelling on a higher, faster vibration, and auric field expands.
5. Spirit needs you to be horizontal in sleep state for the return of your spirit force.
6. Preparation in the body is stimulated by the release of adrenalin, now escorted by Karis.

Tony Blackmore then took us all upon a meditation on illumination, taking us into the higher realms of spirit. The path led us to a minster with high portals and arched ceilings. I sat down in a pew and looked at the stained glass windows with their vibrant colours. There was an archbishop standing in the aisle before the altar dressed in long flowing robes coloured gold, beige, and pink. On his head he wore the bishop's crown.

By the side of him stood a "being" illuminated in white light, dressed in a white gown with long grey hair. He beckoned me forward and embraced me into the white light. I saw purple or violet flowers all around. I then stepped back and felt my doorkeeper behind me. I did not see his face, but I felt his hand brush my face. The sun was shining through the windows, and I felt at peace.

Trance Mediumship with Tony Blackmore 1

Development circle was at Tony Blackmore's home with our regular circle of friends. Tony went into trance, and the doorkeeper came through to each one of us with much laughter and amusing comments. For Sheila, he said it was a good job her brain was not located in her foot. For the instrument, i.e., Tony, he still has work to do on the earth plains. For Neal and Jake, they will both have a long spiritual life and are more family-oriented on the earth plains at the moment.

The doorkeeper stepped back, and Oscar Wilde came through to say that as a group we were advancing on our spiritual paths. He said to Neal that he needed to get on and do the job properly, and then twins would arrive. He also said that it was not important to get married, because it was an invention made by man. (Good luck when telling Ali this!) He said to Jake that the path to spiritualism is a long and lonely road, but as he gets older he would realise that he was on the right path. At this time he had his family to think about and needed to be there for them. For me, he said that I would meet a lady in the near future who was right for me and would lead to fulfilment.

My question to Oscar was about a friend called Sandra who has a blood disorder, and his reply was that the healing she was receiving was for her liver and should have been for her heart. To overcome this, the spirit world would work through me as a channel to heal her by absent healing. This would send turquoise and pink colours to the heart chakra to address the blood disorder. He also said she had a mind-set that was giving her depression and would also require absent healing to the third eye chakra (brow), the colours being silver and gold. He also said that I should speak to her to ask her to pray in the quiet three times so that Spirit would know she wanted them to proceed.

Oscar gave Sheila a message to pass on to the instrument that his condition would be better if he didn't have to take so many pills. The infra-ray treatment would not be beneficial, as it would damage internal organs; the best treatment would be ultrasound.

Oscar then said he was moving back. At this point we thanked him for all he had given us, and the doorkeeper came back to close the door.

This was without doubt a very incredible evening and one when we felt part of the spiritual world.

Trance Mediumship with Tony Blackmore 2

At development circle at Tony Blackmore's home with our regular circle of friends, Tony went into trance and the doorkeeper came through with his usual joviality aimed at Shelia about her choice of dress for the wedding. Her mother didn't like it, but her father did; they also liked the hat. He then spoke to Jake about his giggle and to Neal about smoking his pot to remind us that Spirit knows what we are doing at all times. He said to Mark that he had been through a lot.

Magnuson then came through and said that as a group we were doing well. He spoke about crystals and said that each one of us should have an amethyst, clear quartz, or smoke quartz crystal. We should wash the crystals and place the quartz onto the earth in the garden to restore its energy. He spoke about these crystals and said that we would be working with them through Spirit.

He also talked about the White Brethren and ascension. He told us to look it up and learn all about ascension, as for the next five years, we would be helping people in the western world suffering from social deprivation. He said that all five of us, when we ascend from the earth plains, will be going to fulfil our place in a different part of the universe and that we would not be returning to earth again.

The City of Atlantis was built by godly people, but because of the greed and power of the rulers, the city was destroyed by an earthquake and is buried under the sea in the Gulf Stream.

He then went on to talk about the angel card. Raziel, Angel of Mysteries, inspires us to accept the mystery in all life. His name means "God is my pleasure".

Part 4

Poems and Meditations

Meditation: Atlantis

First of all cleanse yourself of all negative debris within your body. Put it into a black bag and place in the refuse bin outside. You can then proceed to open your chakras and prepare for a meditation with Tony Blackmore.

Holding an amethyst crystal, visualise yourself within a purple pyramid. We are going on a journey back in time to Atlantis, a city lost in time, described as a paradise on earth, peopled by demigods and devastated by a cataclysmic event, such as an earthquake or tidal wave, in a single day and night more than 11,000 years ago.

As you walk out of your pyramid, visualise the ancient buildings and temples, taking note of the style of architecture. Describe the land of flowing fountains, exotic fruits, and canals that enabled a second harvest to be reaped each year.

In the land you can see animals of different species. Make a note of the ones that you recognise, and describe the ones you are not sure of. As you walk around the land, there are many trees with exotic fruits. The colours are varied, and one in particular stands out. What is it?

Not far ahead you can see the sea, so you decide to walk to the beach where you can sit or paddle in the water to feel the energy, listening to the sound of the waves as they roll onto the beach. Describe what you hear.

After a while, you decide to move on to the busy port. Along the way you pass traders selling statues made from stone and crystal pyramids. Also sitting in the shade are many wise teachers in their coloured robes. You can listen to their wisdom. What did they tell you about the city of Atlantis?

As you wander along the street, you come upon a site where men are making pottery and statues. You feel like touching them to connect with the ancient world. You feel visions coming into your mind, and you feel part of them. You are drawn to one in particular, which has a beauty to behold. It is made from marble and has a special significance. What is it?

As the day draws to a close, it is time to walk back to your purple pyramid. Looking up at the night sky, you see the stars forming, and as it gets darker, the Milky Way comes into view. By the time you reach your pyramid, it is completely dark. Once inside the pyramid, you feel refreshed and ready to return to consciousness.

Poem of Love

Such is the love manifests all things beautiful.
We feel it all around us,
Strength that binds us together.
We long for the bonds to remain strong.
What it is to share all things compassionately!
We work at the problems with mutual understanding.
Our feelings for one another cement the partnership.
When we are down, the partner boosts us up.
Our family builds in confidence as they grow.
They mature into adults all too quickly.
Their enthusiasm makes them think they can conquer the world.
When things go wrong, ours is a shoulder to cry on.
We have been there before them and know all the pitfalls.
The one thing they desire that bonds us together
Is love from the heart that keeps us together.

Meditation with the White Brethren

We proceeded and opened up chakras before meditation with Tony Blackmore, which took us on a spiritual journey with the White Brethren.

I walked towards the temple, flanked by my guide and my mother, and entered the temple. In the middle was a small table with a white rose on it. In a semicircle on the other side of the table sat several brethren.

The first brother in the centre got up and came towards me and kissed me on the forehead. Then he returned to his seat. He was dressed in colourful robes with a white cape over his shoulders.

A second brother stood up and opened a leather-bound book on the table. It was coloured crimson. The page that he had opened was blank, and he wrote the word "love" on it. He was a swarthy man and wore a headgear like a turban with different colours and a cloak over his shoulders. His hands were fat with short fingers. His eyes were deep set with bushy eyebrows that were black. He then sat down.

I placed the white rose back on the small table, stepped back, bowed, and walked out of the temple with my guide and my mother onto a golden beach where the sun was shining and the sea was quite calm.

In my hand was an oval-shaped mirror with one handle, edged in gold. I looked into the mirror and saw a dark silhouette, but I could not see the face. It then changed to a side view of my brother David and then to another person, which could have been David when he was younger.

I hurled the mirror into the sea a long way, and then lifted my body up towards the sky. I saw myself flying a Tiger Moth single-engine plane. I was wearing goggles, a leather hat, and a coat, and I was zooming around the sky in and out the white clouds. When I came down, I appeared to be high on a hill overlooking the Cotswold Vale and countryside, admiring the view and thinking how beautiful it all looked.

Meditation for Forgiveness

This meditation with Tony Blackmore is to take a vow and for forgiveness of past experiences with a husband, wife, or partner.

I was walking along a winding path with a stream on the left. Lots of colourful flowers were planted on the way to the temple that was set in the hillside. I walked up the steps through a large wooden door, where I was greeted by an archangel on the left and a high spirit on the right-hand side, surrounded in white light. I then walked forward to a candle holder with a small candle and lit it.

Then I proceeded to a wooden chair in the middle of the aisle, flanked by an archangel and a high spirit on either side. A priest stepped forward with a thin red book and opened it. I placed my gold ring onto the centre of the book, and the priest closed it. I got up and thanked the priest.

We proceeded to walk towards the front door, blowing the candle out on the way. On the right at the door was a pillar box. I opened the door and walked down the steps into a stately home garden with lots of people and beautiful flowers. The sun was shining brightly, and it was very warm as I continued to walk through the garden. I came across a sunflower that was in full bloom and very tall. Quite close by was a table with a picture on it, which some people were looking at, but I could not make out what was in the picture.

Meditation Following a House Clearance

This meditation with Tony Blackmore was to see what we would get as a group, following a friend's house clearance by Tony.

The meditation took us into the countryside. A medieval castle was nearby, surrounded by a moat. The drawbridge in the down position, and the portcullis was open. There was one tower with a flagpole on the top, a St George's Cross on a white background. Some soldiers on the ramparts were moving freely. I walked across the drawbridge into the castle and entered the main hall, where a long table with chairs on either side was situated. Mark was sitting on one side, and the hall was full of people in medieval dress. I sat down opposite Mark and saw a man of swarthy appearance with a turban on his head. He stepped forward and gave Mark a rolled-up scroll. Mark then read out the contents. The man standing behind Mark put his hands on Mark's shoulders. A third man stepped forward from the right and placed an orb with a golden cross on the top in front of Mark. Just then Sheila stepped forward and opened the book on the table and read a reading about Archangel Michael. I then stood up and moved towards a tapestry coloured green and gold. The name Kevin was written on it.

I then took my leave and walked out of the main hall to the outside of the building, where a large lawn was spread out down to a flowing river. There was an old oak chair with a high back and two arm rests. The seat was covered in purple. There was also a fire burning not far from the river, and there was a casket of soil beside the fire. I picked up the casket and sprinkled the soil on the fire to put it out.

A Prayer for Love

We pray for the love of all mankind to manifest in all our ways,
Not to look for greed, jealousy or ill-gotten gains
But to see the good in people in so many ways.
Ours is not to judge or condemn
But to encourage, support, and guide them on their path.
Protect the planet earth, which is a beautiful place
With all the animals, birds and bees, flowers, and all living plants,
Where we can contribute by giving out our love

*By doing so, we shall receive love abundantly in return.
The love that we send out to our families and friends
Is for the love that they gave to us when they were here.
Amen.*

Spring Has Sprung

*Spring has sprung. The first signs of colour have appeared.
The daffodils are all displaying a multitude of yellow.
The snowdrops and the crocuses complete the carpet throughout the gardens.
The violets, so tender and fragile, begin to burst forth.
The bluebells is in flower, and very soon there will be an array
Of blue in many woodland areas.
It is a wonderful time of the year, when the sun shines on all things living.
We ourselves have a spring in our steps. It is the time of year to recharge oneself,
To look forward with enthusiasm at what life will bring us this year.*

ROBERT C SMITH

The Daffodil

Life is like a golden daffodil. Its brightness is illuminating,
So upright and strong is the stem, so regal is the flower.
It withstands the winds and remains steadfast in its prime.
The colours of golden and green are majestic in their combination.
Set in a landscape of trees and grass, they congregate in clusters,
As if to show that they blend with others, forming an array of beauty and splendour.
To understand the personality of the daffodil, one needs only to look at this flower –
To understand the warmth and beauty within, coupled with its strength to survive
In the short time that it is in flower.
All too soon the flower fades, and the foliage goes into decay,
But the bulb remains in the ground to pass the winter.
For in the spring the daffodil comes to life to bloom another year.

Divine Timing by Sue for Robert

Your journey has been long, not only within this life time but also from past encounters. Many lessons have been learned. They enable you to reach this moment in time, whereby the spiritual lessons that have been experienced have culminated to this point of divine timing.

For with each incarnation you choose beforehand, what it is that would benefit your spiritual pathway?

You have grown from a young sapling into a mighty oak with roots firmly set deep into the earth.

Your guides have followed your progress, and it is now that everything is at a point of fruition. Let your branches reach out up to the light, for the power and energy will be given to pass on to others with your healing work. It has been a long journey, but so worthwhile.

The Unicorn by Joseph Panek

Perhaps the most wondrous of all mystical creatures, the unicorn is a symbol of magic, miracles, purity, innocence, and enchantment.

This magical and enchanting animal appears to only a rare few and has the ability to bestow magic and wisdom to those who are pure of heart and virtuous in their deeds.

The presence of a unicorn is announced by the soft and faint tinkling sound of tiny bells being shaken.

As bells and chimes symbolize the presence of divinity, the tinkling sound which accompanies the nearness of a unicorn reminds us that we are in the presence of a highly spiritual essence whose boundless domain encompasses all realms, matter and spirit, pristine knowledge, and wisdom.

The unicorn is depicted as a white horse with a long, straight, spiral-shaped horn protruding from the top of its forehead.

There are three basic symbols contained in the unicorn: the colour white, the horse, and the horn.

The horse is a symbol of travel and movement, and as the unicorn is a spiritual horse, it has the ability to travel and appear wherever and whenever it wishes. It also has the ability to appear throughout all realms and dimensions.

White is the colour of innocence, purity, and perfection, White is symbolically similar to silver, representing the lunar feminine aspects of receptivity, instinct, intuition, and virginity. It is for this reason that to have a unicorn appear to us is both a great honour and a divine gift.

The unicorn's single horn is spiralled, a symbol of the endlessly repeating cycles of time. It is also symbolic of the sword, and the sword symbolizes the mind. The unicorn's horn also signifies unity of thought and purity of reason.

Appendix

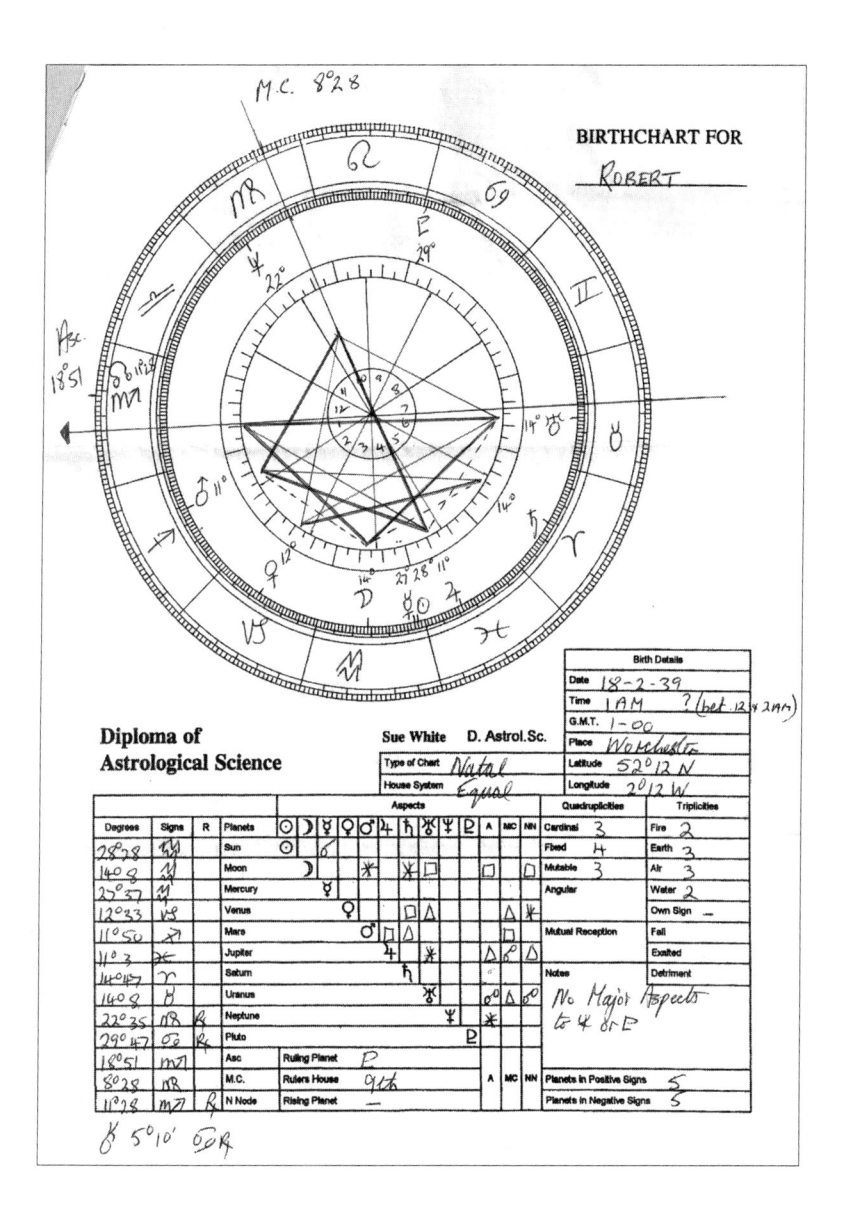

BIRTHCHART FOR Robert

M.C. 8°28

Diploma of Astrological Science — Sue White D. Astrol.Sc.

Type of Chart	Natal
House System	Equal

Birth Details

Date	18-2-39
Time	1 AM ? (bet. 12 & 2 AM)
G.M.T.	1-00
Place	Worcester
Latitude	52°12 N
Longitude	2°12 W

Aspects

Degrees	Signs	R	Planets	☉	☽	☿	♀	♂	♃	♄	♅	♆	♇	A	MC	NN
28°28	♒		Sun	☉	σ											
14°8	♏		Moon		☽		✶		✶	□		□				
2°37	♏		Mercury			☿										
12°33	♑		Venus				♀		□	△			△	✶		
11°50	♐		Mars					♂	□	△				△	♃	△
11°3	♓		Jupiter						♃	✶			△	♃°	△	
14°57	♈		Saturn							♄			°			
14°8	♉		Uranus								♅			0°	△	6°
22°35	♍ R		Neptune								✶	♆		✶		
29°47	♋ R		Pluto										♇			
18°51	♍		Asc	Ruling Planet	♇									A	MC	NN
8°28	♍		M.C.	Rulers House	9th											
11°28	♏ R		N Node	Rising Planet	—											

☽ 5°10' ☉ R

Quadruplicities

Cardinal	3
Fixed	4
Mutable	3
Angular		
Mutual Reception	
Notes	No Major Aspects to ♃ or ♇
Planets in Positive Signs	5
Planets in Negative Signs	5

Triplicities

Fire	2
Earth	3
Air	3
Water	2
Own Sign	—
Fall	
Exalted	
Detriment	

101

Resources

Jeff Powell
Past Life Therapies
www.pastlifetherapies.com

PAPYRUS Prevention of Young Suicide,
Unit 1, Lineva House, 28–32 Milner Street, Warrington, Cheshire, WA5 1AD
Tel 01925 572 444 Mon–Fri 9:00 a.m. to 5:00 p.m.
Email: admin@papyrus-uk.org

HOPELineUK 0800 068 41 41

Maxine Mustoe Spiritualist Medium, Founder, and Guardian of "The Kingdom of Chivronia" in a Nature Spiritualist's Quest
www.psychicmaxine.co.uk

Corinthian Church and Healing Association
An Organisation founded for the furtherance of Spiritual Healing and Spiritual Understanding throughout the World.
www.corinthian-healing.co.uk

Phil Phillips Spiritualist Medium and Healer
http://www.philphillips.no/

Joseph Panek
www.aseekersthoughts.com
Henderson, Nevada

Marcus Burnett, Spiritual Medium and Psychic Artist
Bristol, UK. Email: <u>M.Burnettis1@googlemail.com</u>

Sue Rose, Spiritual Medium
Cheltenham, UK. Email: <u>Suechelt@yahoo.co.uk</u>

Printed in the United States
By Bookmasters